Penultimate Again

Penultimate Again
Morgan Driscoll

Querencia Press – Chicago IL

Q AN IMPRINT OF QUERENCIA PRESS

ISBN 978 1 963943 02 3

.

www.querenciapress.com

First Published in 2024

Querencia Press, LLC
Chicago IL

Printed & Bound in the United States of America

CONTENTS

Penultimate Again

No rock that falls from space
exploding—
friction-ed, in the vanished air.
No child's foot, slipper-soft,
brushed along the fireflies.
No panicked mob that runs to
ruin,
or fallen flower pulled from a
lapel.
No cinema, no sin,
this just in:

A man wipes his spectacles;
traffic sounds;
another day begins.

6:00am
6:30am
7:00am
7:30am
8:00am
8:30am
9:00am
9:30am
10:00am
10:30am
11:00am
11:30am
12:00pm
12:30pm
1:00pm
1:30pm
2:00pm
2:30pm
3:00pm
3:30pm
4:00pm
4:30pm
5:00pm
5:30pm
6:00pm
6:30pm
7:00pm
7:30pm
8:00pm
8:30pm
9:00pm
9:30pm
10:00pm
10:30pm
11:00pm
11:30pm
12:00am

6:00am
6:30am
7:00am
7:30am
8:00am
8:30am
9:00am
9:30am
10:00am
10:30am
11:00am
11:30am
12:00pm
12:30pm
1:00pm
1:30pm
2:00pm
2:30pm
3:00pm
3:30pm
4:00pm
4:30pm
5:00pm
5:30pm
6:00pm
6:30pm
7:00pm
7:30pm
8:00pm
8:30pm
9:00pm
9:30pm
10:00pm
10:30pm
11:00pm
11:30pm
12:00am

NY Minute

I stand in the street
no cars, just sun
blazing off the early oiled tar,
my wrists extended like offerings.

Take the blood that moves
below the skin,
red. Like the dawn
that barely warms this winter Sunday.

Take it, fill it with light,
leach corruption
from nighttime furies:
the heat that will not keep.

I smell the blinding steam
that rises through
the scent of wants
discarded, met and sallow,

and heave oblations;
snatched from Dionysus
strewn to Apollo.

Brunch to follow.

Freak Accident

Left leg wobbled as the right foot missed the pant leg;
big toe caught on belt loop, double hop then topple
of two hundred thirteen pounds of father flesh, soft
to coffee table glass, hard iron wrought in curly-cues,
purchased on a whim in copper hues one affluent morning
long ago. Down he goes, head crashing as a calloused heel
lofts the weighted leg with denim webbing off
its recently mistaken confidence,
temple smashing with one hundred shards,
his last thought, profanely, of no consequence.

One can see the humor in his grownup children's tragedy,
inconvenienced progeny, sifting through the passwords
and what's left of the once ample bank accounts,
haggling with the woman found, finally for love.
Ambiguity was a precious thing to keep the peace
as he negotiated through the years he thought
were ample too. What are they to do? The kids? The wife?
They'll just live a normal life, progressively giggling
more and more, at what Thanksgivings remain—
one can hope.

6:00am
6:30am
7:00am
7:30am
8:00am
8:30am
9:00am
9:30am
10:00am
10:30am
11:00am
11:30am
12:00pm
12:30pm
1:00pm
1:30pm
2:00pm
2:30pm
3:00pm
3:30pm
4:00pm
4:30pm
5:00pm
5:30pm
6:00pm
6:30pm
7:00pm
7:30pm
8:00pm
8:30pm
9:00pm
9:30pm
10:00pm
10:30pm
11:00pm
11:30pm
12:00am

Morning Drive, After An Ice Storm

Wires glistening,
windows rimed,
laden limbs
perched above the school-bus stops,
we're blinded as on any other blazing morning—
only more so now with this refraction through
ten thousand icy trees.

"A Winter Wonderland"
clichés my tween,
with so few words prepared,
his first time seeing
a forest made of glass
and woven crystal.

"It catches in my throat and almost chokes"
I want to say to him,
"this captured light
which never could be caught in words...
imprisoned sun,
which glints off ridge for miles.
And jumps from inch to inch...
a frozen glow that slides
from branch to branch,
and leans into the sparkling road
and only lasts till lunchtime at the latest
when it finally can reclaim a little warmth and drip from
twigs,
weeping
like the way I feel this moment."

But really,
"winter-wonder" works as well
as any other word to reach for
when saying what can not be said,
and so I ask if he's remembered
his winter hat
instead.

Frost Morning

Follow me
into those razor trees that cut
the bluff beyond
but are also cut
by sunlight slanting from too soon a sky.
We can fly
above the barren twigs and dive
into the arid air, frigid
with the frozen branch,
forgotten leaf, and scratch,
and disaffection.

When I reflect on how
I often feel despair despite
these times of brutal clarity;
imagined as a falcon or a hawk above,
amidst, the hibernating branches
hard with both familiar form
and sublime peculiarity,
I shudder with short sighted anguish
twisting into sudden glee
and wish,
to bend a tangled I
into a simple we.
Follow me.

6:00am
6:30am
7:00am
7:30am
8:00am
8:30am
9:00am
9:30am
10:00am
10:30am
11:00am
11:30am
12:00pm
12:30pm
1:00pm
1:30pm
2:00pm
2:30pm
3:00pm
3:30pm
4:00pm
4:30pm
5:00pm
5:30pm
6:00pm
6:30pm
7:00pm
7:30pm
8:00pm
8:30pm
9:00pm
9:30pm
10:00pm
10:30pm
11:00pm
11:30pm
12:00am

Everyday Embrace

There was a first, and has to be
a last, to last forever when forever comes;
but this one here, this wordless kiss
so fast—this brushing as we pass
will just be numbered "everyday embrace"
as gracefully you disengage, continue
with this chore or that concern.
I face what's next to see to on this day
of nothing grand, save your brushed living
in this house with me—bemused
at finding out so late that muse is not—
an anguished fate, a sin, the sleep I lose—
it's just berceuse; chimed wind and whistled pot,
a lulling hum, a whispered thought or charm;
a solace in your firm enfolding arms.

Grounded

It was umbers burnt and raw beneath the breathing stems.
It was siennas, ochers,
mocha roots weaving through the charcoal soil,
the caramel mulch,
the taupe and tan and tawny leaves dying since the fall.
It was worms,
with cordovan skin coursing
through the olive moss,
the dappled light glinting with the wind.
It was: loamy hands, clay beneath the nails,
seedlings gently placed beneath the earth.
It was the pruning of the plants that mustn't grow;
the ordinary choosing.
It was these then,

not:
the siren inflorescence of the petals,
intoxication of the ruttish air,
infatuation of the pistils and the anthers,
the blooming.

It was this:
the thousand shades of sand and dirt,
ten thousand shades of common earth,
the countless choices needing to be made, most of all
the nurture,
that brought him day by day
again to tend,
to husband.

6:00am
6:30am
7:00am
7:30am
8:00am
8:30am
9:00am
9:30am
10:00am
10:30am
11:00am
11:30am
12:00pm
12:30pm
1:00pm
1:30pm
2:00pm
2:30pm
3:00pm
3:30pm
4:00pm
4:30pm
5:00pm
5:30pm
6:00pm
6:30pm
7:00pm
7:30pm
8:00pm
8:30pm
9:00pm
9:30pm
10:00pm
10:30pm
11:00pm
11:30pm
12:00am

6:00am
6:30am
7:00am
7:30am
8:00am
8:30am
9:00am
9:30am
10:00am
10:30am
11:00am
11:30am
12:00pm
12:30pm
1:00pm
1:30pm
2:00pm
2:30pm
3:00pm
3:30pm
4:00pm
4:30pm
5:00pm
5:30pm
6:00pm
6:30pm
7:00pm
7:30pm
8:00pm
8:30pm
9:00pm
9:30pm
10:00pm
10:30pm
11:00pm
11:30pm
12:00am

November Birches

Leaves have mostly left
falling into yellow mulch,
and branches are bereft—
bitter breeze has been indulged.

Scratched plans of canon architects,
papered trunks that bend and mold
cathedral trees are dark abscess,
a tangled, hallowed forest cold

with whistled prayers, frigid as a foreign sun
—weak and white in icy sky. They cry
alien and high above the whipping mass
of twigs and trunks.

Nothing is at rest—the wind
is from the west, and cold between
the quavering conifers
which contrast with the stubborn birch

preparing for the snow and ice
to numb and consecrate and hide.
They bide, and they refuse to die
in this chance, unlikely church.

Carpe Lingo

Easy to climb...the white pine,
needles soft on knees, a breeze
to scramble up, the branches-more
than any tree should need but
there they are...to cradle while
you breathe and breathe the blue above
announcing through the greens "come up,
come up to here and see, and hear
and seize a moment you might work a little for";
above the forest floor,
above the trunks and twigs, the pointed leaves
above the dark, confounding trees,
higher, higher, come,
come to be.

6:00am
6:30am
7:00am
7:30am
8:00am
8:30am
9:00am
9:30am
10:00am
10:30am
11:00am
11:30am
12:00pm
12:30pm
1:00pm
1:30pm
2:00pm
2:30pm
3:00pm
3:30pm
4:00pm
4:30pm
5:00pm
5:30pm
6:00pm
6:30pm
7:00pm
7:30pm
8:00pm
8:30pm
9:00pm
9:30pm
10:00pm
10:30pm
11:00pm
11:30pm
12:00am

6:00am
6:30am
7:00am
7:30am
8:00am
8:30am
9:00am
9:30am
10:00am
10:30am
11:00am
11:30am
12:00pm
12:30pm
1:00pm
1:30pm
2:00pm
2:30pm
3:00pm
3:30pm
4:00pm
4:30pm
5:00pm
5:30pm
6:00pm
6:30pm
7:00pm
7:30pm
8:00pm
8:30pm
9:00pm
9:30pm
10:00pm
10:30pm
11:00pm
11:30pm
12:00am

Breeding

There is a pear tree in the middle of the dog park
and like St. Augustine I want a pear
because I want a pear. There is no one near.
The dogs all whim around the edges of the park,
dash across the ladies in the shade of the gazebo.
My dog
splashes all the water from communal dishes.
What a naughty dog she is. Yet I feel shame
in scoping-out this public pear tree.

There is no one who approaches but
the raucous dogs, who sniff
and hump and furl their primal selves,
and me. The dogs are as free as these pears
are free for my craving. They're as free as acting brazenly,
like I don't really mind who see's desire on display.

In the days of Reformation, Luther said "sin boldly!"
and here I am on toes to pull
a leaf to grab a branch to grasp a fruit
in clumsy fingertips.
No one knows the kind of strain it is,
for me, trying to act so naturally.
No one seems to care as well,
they mind their dogs and chat among themselves.
You'd think behaving like a normal human being
might not be enough to send a man to hell.
"Bad dog!, Leave it there!" I yell.

Consolation Prize

Overdressed, as if attending my own mother's funeral:
dark suit, dark shoes, tie;
I wish for rain, stare through silent windows, sigh;
and turn the engine. I begin the drive

to my own mother's funeral, in a dented gray van;
high miles, low bluebook, vague plan
forming to replace it with inheritance.
Mom would understand

this pattern of spending what I do not yet have were she
not cold, quiet, gently boxed,
attending her own funeral. She loved me,
would give me cash or sell some stocks

again and again, freeing funds for a prodigal son:
wasteful, reckless, wanton
in habit and decision. I had loved her so
but still need money while consoled

here in dark condolence clothes.
There are expenses to pay,
pallbearer, casket, hearse, grave,
but most of all, the mess I've made

for years,
as I've known someday I'd be here
on my own,
at my own mother's funeral.

6:00am
6:30am
7:00am
7:30am
8:00am
8:30am
9:00am
9:30am
10:00am
10:30am
11:00am
11:30am
12:00pm
12:30pm
1:00pm
1:30pm
2:00pm
2:30pm
3:00pm
3:30pm
4:00pm
4:30pm
5:00pm
5:30pm
6:00pm
6:30pm
7:00pm
7:30pm
8:00pm
8:30pm
9:00pm
9:30pm
10:00pm
10:30pm
11:00pm
11:30pm
12:00am

Stimulated Economy

High above
and in between the tropics
on the darker continents ignored
or mostly ignored in the places
where the latte's poured,
the coffee cherries, picked and sorted,
prepped to dry,
lie on endless tables, open meshed and raised,
placed by hands rarely asked their age
paid at almost $2.00 per day

And now in burlap bags,
twine tightened to a mountain ass,
splattered with mud and puddled sun,
as rains pass late
in November days;
now as bags of beans
descending to be milled
then piled into cargo holds,
spilled green into the roaster plants,
then ground and steamed into my Venti Drip.
I toss the tattooed teen my change; an almost $2.00 tip.

Zephyr Hair

Billow thin, so fair,
on wind and floating
in the garden groves,
on garden scent since,
fathers had a daughter,
since a daughter laughed
in dogwood, since the first time
that you noticed blossoms drifting
in the breezing blondie blue and cotton,
puffy tufts of shouts announcing "here, I'm here, I'm bursty here!"
In leaps and streaming in the wafty playground air.

6:00am
6:30am
7:00am
7:30am
8:00am
8:30am
9:00am
9:30am
10:00am
10:30am
11:00am
11:30am
12:00pm
12:30pm
1:00pm
1:30pm
2:00pm
2:30pm
3:00pm
3:30pm
4:00pm
4:30pm
5:00pm
5:30pm
6:00pm
6:30pm
7:00pm
7:30pm
8:00pm
8:30pm
9:00pm
9:30pm
10:00pm
10:30pm
11:00pm
11:30pm
12:00am

She Asked for Yellow

They are saying Kaddish
but I can't understand
in this room of family and friends so young—
where I am a stranger hearing words planned

at the hospice only yesterday.
Ancient syllables pass
through morning light and pass
through a tide of yellow because she asked.

I don't know this girl who died,
who asked for yellow
in our sleeves, and in our kerchiefs,
and in old ties worn, as voices echo

through dusted light, on children
who mourn and learn to mourn.
I am just acquaintance for a sudden task
visiting some friends, just summoned to learn

of service at the synagogue,
and shiva at the home.
I can't translate through the chants
but for yisrael, but for shalom,

I can't but I hear amen,
in men's breath, on women's sighs;
a blessing, a confusion, through adolescents
wearing clothes perhaps a size

too small, or dug from attics, but wearing
yellow somewhere because she asked.
In unison the sounds:
Yitgadal v'yitkadash,

I can't understand, so I glance
outside, spotting butterflies
alit and yellow,
on a darkened mid-March branch.

22

Father's Ashes, Boxed And Stashed

Put me in a vase, or buy an urn
for heaven's sake. You owe me that
at least. I've earned a daily thought or two
for giving you a life, and laughs or two.
Could you let me see a bit of shadow overhead
or listen to a distant muffled grandkid?

I made you with your mom, I thought
of England while it happened or
some English chap perhaps; the point
I want to make: I made you through
a sense of duty. Don't you think that
sheathing me in plastic shirks your own?

And shoved behind some books my God
that's cruel, you knew how much
I love to read and left me here week
after year, through months with the dust
for a decade as dust, in a carton in a bag
and the Sharpied word "dad"

You try your best you say, to get me to
that northern place I loved and hoped
that you would love. You'll give me
back to sun and air; a private shaken
toss you say you hope will be a final rest.
What does it mean to try your best?

6:00am
6:30am
7:00am
7:30am
8:00am
8:30am
9:00am
9:30am
10:00am
10:30am
11:00am
11:30am
12:00pm
12:30pm
1:00pm
1:30pm
2:00pm
2:30pm
3:00pm
3:30pm
4:00pm
4:30pm
5:00pm
5:30pm
6:00pm
6:30pm
7:00pm
7:30pm
8:00pm
8:30pm
9:00pm
9:30pm
10:00pm
10:30pm
11:00pm
11:30pm
12:00am

Guessing Biography At The Estate Sale

No woman ever owned that patterned chair of
clipper ships and tavern signs,
or that Royal Doulton Mug of Sherlock Holmes.
It's mostly men, collecting vintage Underwoods,
neon beer signs,
wooden shelves of leather bound whatevers.
How many shot glasses could one man keep?

I'm going with long time divorced,
twenty years to make the house you thought you wanted.
The oak and brass and captains chairs,
the solid things.
So many oils of painted pheasants hanging on the walls.
Your wife had kept the house you really loved and antique
silver,
your lawyers won for you: some indulgence over time.

What did grandkids do when forced to come;
their parents ever watching you for signs of age?
You'd find their finger marks atop the dusty beer steins
or aborted pillow forts inside the den,
—the result of disappointment with your too few quilts
and shams.
"Papa was ok, he gave us cash," you hoped they'd say,
when they were old enough to have their own memories.

And that's where you had been these passing years.
Reminiscing colleague and accomplishment,
learning lonely and happy could be the same thing.
She took all her lace and her doilies
but you found items that had been deferred.
You had hoped that she'd miss you, but not really,
no one should be sad for dessert.

24

Baroque Rain With Coffee

—in conversation with Smoke by Dorianna Laux

You think it's Bach.
It should be but it's not;
it's some forgotten composer called
Marcello with his oboes lifting tear drops,
just before they form on cheekbones pointing
at the rain—windows gray as wired screening,
but it's not. It's just the rain which moves
as slow as coffee, black and still it moves
in little trills of light and gray, reflecting
swaying time and oboes weeping
in a lonely day remembered like this day
but only long ago and also yesterday's adagio
when nothing mattered but the next thing
and the next and next. It's so much gray and yet
it's so sublime, you suck in air like sobbing,
but your head is clear, your hands are warm
and cupped around a mug of coffee, bitter as a slight,
as crystalline as slaps delivered undeserved
amidst your signaled virtue. Crows peck in the wet
and oboes play and coffee drips and sips and
all the day is gone and all you have are chef-kissed
darkened thoughts and pleasures of it doesn't matter
but the little things you choose, and thanking
God, who isn't there, she's chosen you.

6:00am
6:30am
7:00am
7:30am
8:00am
8:30am
9:00am
9:30am
10:00am
10:30am
11:00am
11:30am
12:00pm
12:30pm
1:00pm
1:30pm
2:00pm
2:30pm
3:00pm
3:30pm
4:00pm
4:30pm
5:00pm
5:30pm
6:00pm
6:30pm
7:00pm
7:30pm
8:00pm
8:30pm
9:00pm
9:30pm
10:00pm
10:30pm
11:00pm
11:30pm
12:00am

Outside The Diner

Watch the blonde
trot down the ramp,
down past the steam
that leaks through kitchen vents.
See her clench
her arms against
December as
she bends to rolling windows.
The car is late,
the driver shouts
excuses to
a scowl not very blonde indeed;
a fog of fatalism smokes the air
as angry shoulders challenge,
then concede.

Impact Of War

Boneyard leaking bones
till shifting rivers,
tilting hummocks
tilling plows of oxen
turned to tractor,
turned to combine;
pull the last remaining shrined remains
and leave the now unhallowed soil
to rest in peace.

6:00am
6:30am
7:00am
7:30am
8:00am
8:30am
9:00am
9:30am
10:00am
10:30am
11:00am
11:30am
12:00pm
12:30pm
1:00pm
1:30pm
2:00pm
2:30pm
3:00pm
3:30pm
4:00pm
4:30pm
5:00pm
5:30pm
6:00pm
6:30pm
7:00pm
7:30pm
8:00pm
8:30pm
9:00pm
9:30pm
10:00pm
10:30pm
11:00pm
11:30pm
12:00am

Thou Hast Taught Me To Say

The Brandeis University Oppressive Language List
suggests substituting the phrase, "content note" for the
phrase, "trigger warning".

My words of offense have been placed in the scuttle,
ignited, then tossed, hod and all, to Ghenna.

Still, my good intentions lay dwarfed
by what remains in my implied iniquity.

My nouns lie gendered and unrepentant
I am emasculated by my pronouns which lay unchecked.

Chief among my sins are my synonyms.

Crippled by grief but not rightly so.
Handicapped by blindness, I wander
in dark and black and am lost.

I seek new orientation but do not keep straight
—only narrow, and yet only now have learned
that queerness can be warranted.

None of my friends happen to be anything,
nor do they suffer things —they only have them
—except for fools.

I have held my oxymorons as absurd
but have learned that they are genius, in a different way.

I cannibalize integrity by feasting on exotic fare.

Yea, I have been miserly with the words I have censored
and shamed in my desire to end all bigotry.

Surely I shall proceed with the words of the wise
and the sayings of the aged will remain unsaid.

Artificial Intelligence

The last time at the office of the otolaryngologist,
I had smartly typed my next appointment
promptly on my smart phone screen
at the same time it was read to me
by the lovely admin,
Marcie;
who said to me today,
when I arrived right at noon
as my clever schedule told me to,
that I had missed my meeting with the doctor
and clearly someone must have erred, but not her.

6:00am
6:30am
7:00am
7:30am
8:00am
8:30am
9:00am
9:30am
10:00am
10:30am
11:00am
11:30am
12:00pm
12:30pm
1:00pm
1:30pm
2:00pm
2:30pm
3:00pm
3:30pm
4:00pm
4:30pm
5:00pm
5:30pm
6:00pm
6:30pm
7:00pm
7:30pm
8:00pm
8:30pm
9:00pm
9:30pm
10:00pm
10:30pm
11:00pm
11:30pm
12:00am

On The Internet No One Knows

I'm just a dog
laid down on porches
simple
in my sun and shade.
A good boy
wanting nothing but
this moment. I'm a dog
that snaps at the affronting thing
enraged
at the atrocity that passed
my guarded eyes.
A dog who chases
with his jaws
a tail misunderstood
with circled fury, doggedly
pursuing all my rabid hates,
my desperate needs with need
to show my teeth and need to show
my whitened furious eyes.
I only need

to lie here in the dappled shade
and mottled light
and be completely free
from any sort of feeling that
you might be right.

Listening To A Love Poem
25 Years After Writing It

yes
I do love you
but want to not
and turn away
to small success
and run through rooms
where you might be
and scattered glances
like campfire sparks
alight,
ignite,
a tinder heart.

yes
the desires were entitled
I thought your flesh might save me
and turn away
the pathos
and pretending
where you might be
a muse excusing infidelity
and predation
could not exist in poetry.
Ignite
these lies to cinders
I was common
not goddamn Byron

6:00am
6:30am
7:00am
7:30am
8:00am
8:30am
9:00am
9:30am
10:00am
10:30am
11:00am
11:30am
12:00pm
12:30pm
1:00pm
1:30pm
2:00pm
2:30pm
3:00pm
3:30pm
4:00pm
4:30pm
5:00pm
5:30pm
6:00pm
6:30pm
7:00pm
7:30pm
8:00pm
8:30pm
9:00pm
9:30pm
10:00pm
10:30pm
11:00pm
11:30pm
12:00am

Alone. Alive.

It really is quiet: this quiet forest—
slow sound eaten by branches, and leaves,
quick sound by the foggy sky.
Drifting mist surrounds the face
that floats here in the mist
the deer
the toad
my face that drifts amidst
the darkening trunks, against the tired loam,
and in decaying gray.
The undergrowth is sparse and roots are hard,
standing here is easy though.

I wish that everywhere I go were like this place,
that everyplace was where there was no time
to count the time, and hours passed as fast
as dew drops on a spiders web, as slow
as fog below the fallen tree
across forgotten stoney walls.

Were it Fall, my feet would stand on carnival
and sunlight come some 90 million miles;
would scream in carny barks off leaves
about to die not quite.
If Spring, my mouth would taste
a magic green, would screech
with short-lived petal pinks and whites
and all the colors minus blue which rules
the canopy regardless.
Summer/Winter have their dramas too,
but this, this in between
of brown and beige, ecru
dark forest green that glints obsidian;
this time of no one on the trail
no barks or cries of mystery in distance
or even thud of branch
against the cradling mulch—
I hope an afterlife is such
I hope that heaven is this much.

So Many Roses

The only thing stirring was the spoon
that was thrumming through wrinkled tea.
We sat—bone china service sitting
gentle on lace and improvised space
in mother's taut parlor.

Filled with liquor, father's cabinet
closed with dust these twenty years
brought my sister's shift of weight,
I saw her eyes raise from the spoon
remaining still but for the stirring.

Anything is better than this sifted silence
even shredded memories
of our father dead, transgressions never healed,
and mom who kept the cabinet sealed
until this week, right to her dying day.
"Does anybody want a drink?" I say.

6:00am
6:30am
7:00am
7:30am
8:00am
8:30am
9:00am
9:30am
10:00am
10:30am
11:00am
11:30am
12:00pm
12:30pm
1:00pm
1:30pm
2:00pm
2:30pm
3:00pm
3:30pm
4:00pm
4:30pm
5:00pm
5:30pm
6:00pm
6:30pm
7:00pm
7:30pm
8:00pm
8:30pm
9:00pm
9:30pm
10:00pm
10:30pm
11:00pm
11:30pm
12:00am

33

Last Call

There were splinters
and dock wood slippery
from deep waters, mountain cold.
There were the boys,
they moved without our fear.
Their joys circled jumping, plunging, sprints.
Circled like snows on the ridges holding the blues,
the sapphires, lazulines,
the forest tree greens, which might as well be blue:
they melted lake to hill to sky.
There was danger, but there was laughter.
And there was some peace
between us.
There was a day in July.

Around The Cape Of Good Hope

Western wind embillowed this
ship sails on an open sea
that swallows lesser vessels;
she,
emboldened by surviving the
surprise of sudden squalls, now sways
atop the fraying waves
and dips
below a swell that curls
above a surging tide;
and now
without a place to hide
inside a wilderness of wild
whitecapped surf
she rides along the spume
towards line of sea and sky
and navigates as best she can
what looms an empty vector pointing all ways
having long abandoned chart or plan.

6:00am
6:30am
7:00am
7:30am
8:00am
8:30am
9:00am
9:30am
10:00am
10:30am
11:00am
11:30am
12:00pm
12:30pm
1:00pm
1:30pm
2:00pm
2:30pm
3:00pm
3:30pm
4:00pm
4:30pm
5:00pm
5:30pm
6:00pm
6:30pm
7:00pm
7:30pm
8:00pm
8:30pm
9:00pm
9:30pm
10:00pm
10:30pm
11:00pm
11:30pm
12:00am

Matryoshka Metaphor
In The Discourse
Between Quantum Uncertainty
And Nonsense Verse

How obscure—
to start a poem this way
—almost ensure
most audience is gone
and will not even read this far,
while just a few delay,
turning the impatient page.

And now, having made it down
to here, you're suspicious I've
misused your time with
stupid use of meta lines,
insipid rhymes referring
to referring to referring.
What is meta for anyway?

You're a doll, really, a peach,
for sticking with me on this;
like a barnacle with grit
or something similar
to peaches having reached
this point not knowing
if there is a point continuing;

like a man who tried to build
a breadbox that
was bigger than a breadbox.
But suppose we might be living in
a box inside a box
inside a box atop
a stack of turtles made

of particles entangled
that are anywhere but where
you think, until you think.
Then if thinking's what it takes
to make a thing a thing,
it might be there is nothing
that makes a poem worth...

36

Quiet Recognitions

When distant wishes calling you
in breezes rushing off the bay,
return, as blush of deja vu,
of distant whisper calling you
to kisses spent at twenty two
which purchase now this windswept day:
insistent whispers hushing you
with breezes, shushing off the bay.

This shallow bay whose frozen salt
and sea grass mounded on the beach
from winter wind which howls and halts
the shallow bay whose blowing salt
turns words that it was no one's fault
to whispers muted each to each.
This shallow bay, with frozen salt
and sea grass mounded on the beach.

Our yearling years, in early March
embraced and braced against the cold
and facing futures by and large
from yearling years in early March
that won't contain the burning torch
we feel can singe us till we're old
past yearling years in early March
embraced and braced against the cold.

If distant wishes call to her
in distant breezes where she may
be standing on the sand somewhere
perhaps resistant and dismissive there
to daydreams blowing in the air
I hope she sees just yesterday
for me, were kisses that we shared;
distant breezes, off the bay.

6:00am
6:30am
7:00am
7:30am
8:00am
8:30am
9:00am
9:30am
10:00am
10:30am
11:00am
11:30am
12:00pm
12:30pm
1:00pm
1:30pm
2:00pm
2:30pm
3:00pm
3:30pm
4:00pm
4:30pm
5:00pm
5:30pm
6:00pm
6:30pm
7:00pm
7:30pm
8:00pm
8:30pm
9:00pm
9:30pm
10:00pm
10:30pm
11:00pm
11:30pm
12:00am

6:00am
6:30am
7:00am
7:30am
8:00am
8:30am
9:00am
9:30am
10:00am
10:30am
11:00am
11:30am
12:00pm
12:30pm
1:00pm
1:30pm
2:00pm
2:30pm
3:00pm
3:30pm
4:00pm
4:30pm
5:00pm
5:30pm
6:00pm
6:30pm
7:00pm
7:30pm
8:00pm
8:30pm
9:00pm
9:30pm
10:00pm
10:30pm
11:00pm
11:30pm
12:00am

Freshman Drop-Off

This van, this road,
—I've rode a thousand times.
It all looks different now somehow
—I try and curl in fitful dreams,
back here, behind the driver's seat.
In front, I see my son asleep,
another passenger like me,
his feet hiked on the dashboard of
this dented Odyssey.

His mother—soon an ex-wife
—drives fierce in dawning countryside
her impatience with the miles—
the same intensity that's driven me away.
I stay silent, fitted in the back between
the duffle bags of bedding,
the mini fridge, the clothing,
that he came to wear so stylishly
so suddenly.

We ride
the thirteen midwest hours,
eighteen years to get us here,
four more left to watch familiar knots
slip and let us slip into
re-braided memories, or new.

We manage to produce a few I think
we'll choose to keep
by taking turns, we three, behind
impartial steering wheel, discussing
favorite episodes, disobeying
traffic code along prolific barley corn,
in deepening Ohio.

She and I, we try
and hold our tongues for some civility
but more, as audience hush so that,
within this shortening time, we might
get to hear him speak a few more lines,
his part—
branching to its own dramatic arc.

38

Uncomposed

By the lake,
which laps the air with solitude
and teases silence,
you take a photo of nightfall blue
reflecting with a waning moon
from the surface.

And I am there,
reflecting near the lake in twilight,
regretting silence. I'm
outside the field of your focus,
next to you as you expose an image
on the surface...

but not for real.
Real is the falcon's folded
silence in the lake
shore shadow watching, with
strobe light freezing sharply
off the surface

of one eye.
In growing coldness, raptor like,
ignoring silence I
startle you by clapping echoes off the lake
side, dark, snapping into memory
when the quiet
was surfeit.

6:00am
6:30am
7:00am
7:30am
8:00am
8:30am
9:00am
9:30am
10:00am
10:30am
11:00am
11:30am
12:00pm
12:30pm
1:00pm
1:30pm
2:00pm
2:30pm
3:00pm
3:30pm
4:00pm
4:30pm
5:00pm
5:30pm
6:00pm
6:30pm
7:00pm
7:30pm
8:00pm
8:30pm
9:00pm
9:30pm
10:00pm
10:30pm
11:00pm
11:30pm
12:00am

6:00am
6:30am
7:00am
7:30am
8:00am
8:30am
9:00am
9:30am
10:00am
10:30am
11:00am
11:30am
12:00pm
12:30pm
1:00pm
1:30pm
2:00pm
2:30pm
3:00pm
3:30pm
4:00pm
4:30pm
5:00pm
5:30pm
6:00pm
6:30pm
7:00pm
7:30pm
8:00pm
8:30pm
9:00pm
9:30pm
10:00pm
10:30pm
11:00pm
11:30pm
12:00am

53 Charter Oak Lane. Parents Party, Pre-Limo.

The pink shirts fit as I do not.
Trouser creases:
plumb lines in a renovated kitchen.
My denim sags at the knees.
Their patio shades with Juneberry leaves,
as we move to move outside, shall we?

Our boys are in tuxedos.
They fret corsages
that are snapped,
in transparent plastic cases.
They are guarded, but sincerely josh,
above their eager bowties.

The girls arrive in gowns too lithe
for any but a fashion model,
or well to do sixteen year old.
They take and give the social cues I didn't have at sixteen,
and sometimes lack at sixty,
but falter at the pinning of the boutonniere.

My son is thin and tall. So tall.
He dances through the hormones and the facile cheer
with no need to prove that he belongs here.
The hostess, tucked and trim, smiles, as if that were true
for me.
She offers me a Chardonnay.
The Husbands murmur Real Estate.

I shift to find a place to wait, and watch my son.
From shadow.

Re-reading My Bucket List

Sky diving of course,
boring, pro-forma, apt.
But way too much travel for just 30 years max:
sometimes I can't bother to walk to the kitchen.

Still, so much I haven't seen.
Taj Mahal, Great Wall,
the world's largest twine ball in Kansas,
not a well lived life, I guess, without these.

A poem in the New Yorker,
hiking the A-T,
dawn on Denali, brewing campfire coffee.
Had I considered that I'd be that guy I'd hate to meet?

And what is it about the edges of things?
Tristan da Cunha, St. Kilda Isle west of the outer
Hebrides; why so important to walk on the places so few
have been?
It's like I'm trying for some sort of distinction,

while this list should be written, by definition,
only for me.
It reads like it's slanted towards noteworthy things
for others to say at the eulogy.

And would it kill me if I didn't do
these things before I die?
If it stayed just like this, memories of them,
laughing with her,

I think I'd be alright.

6:00am
6:30am
7:00am
7:30am
8:00am
8:30am
9:00am
9:30am
10:00am
10:30am
11:00am
11:30am
12:00pm
12:30pm
1:00pm
1:30pm
2:00pm
2:30pm
3:00pm
3:30pm
4:00pm
4:30pm
5:00pm
5:30pm
6:00pm
6:30pm
7:00pm
7:30pm
8:00pm
8:30pm
9:00pm
9:30pm
10:00pm
10:30pm
11:00pm
11:30pm
12:00am

6:00am
6:30am
7:00am
7:30am
8:00am
8:30am
9:00am
9:30am
10:00am
10:30am
11:00am
11:30am
12:00pm
12:30pm
1:00pm
1:30pm
2:00pm
2:30pm
3:00pm
3:30pm
4:00pm
4:30pm
5:00pm
5:30pm
6:00pm
6:30pm
7:00pm
7:30pm
8:00pm
8:30pm
9:00pm
9:30pm
10:00pm
10:30pm
11:00pm
11:30pm
12:00am

Clearly

The long stem glass is waiting
to be broken, shattered
on the porcelain, fallen
from the high shelf on tippy toes.
Gestured with staunch points

subsequent, it
will have had an accident as
someone examines
remains of once gifted wedding sets.

Filmy with soap, it slips invisible,
crystal into hot ammonia water shallow
thud against a dinner plate.
The long stem glass is not broken
yet— still resonates into cabinet corners,
tinks cheers to pairs. Its shards

are impatient to be hidden in the rug.
The stem dreams of hilts and sabers,
the goblet only of shanks as it sits
on lips that sip chilled chardonnay

—so cold the glass has misted
to a squeaky finger fog. It sings
in burgundy, cabernet. Rosé waits
quiet under rose bouquet, inevitable
towards some regret and carpet stain.

The Confessional Poet Hits A Wall

Did you really look for thunderclaps written on your
sleeve;
or think that you'd seduce Euterpe with a need to self
deceive,
or cast a spell of language with some sexual proclivity?
Everyone's the same—a bit, and no-one gives a shit about
your fetid peccadillos.
Who doesn't have their turpitude
and rectitude to winnow?
Who cares about the wheat and chaff?
How about a little hope, or even just a laugh?

Now there's nothing left to tell—no transgressions to
confess.
The meter and the rhyme's still there, but nothing's left for
content.
It's all been told; the crushing sin, the petty vice, the
thoughts within
you wish you hadn't had, but had to broadcast
nonetheless.
It's all been used as ballast in a quest for lyric,
unsuppressed
and unsurpassed perhaps. It's all been blabbed, now all
you have,
is the slightly useful skill-set of remaining unembarrassed.

6:00am
6:30am
7:00am
7:30am
8:00am
8:30am
9:00am
9:30am
10:00am
10:30am
11:00am
11:30am
12:00pm
12:30pm
1:00pm
1:30pm
2:00pm
2:30pm
3:00pm
3:30pm
4:00pm
4:30pm
5:00pm
5:30pm
6:00pm
6:30pm
7:00pm
7:30pm
8:00pm
8:30pm
9:00pm
9:30pm
10:00pm
10:30pm
11:00pm
11:30pm
12:00am

6:00am
6:30am
7:00am
7:30am
8:00am
8:30am
9:00am
9:30am
10:00am
10:30am
11:00am
11:30am
12:00pm
12:30pm
1:00pm
1:30pm
2:00pm
2:30pm
3:00pm
3:30pm
4:00pm
4:30pm
5:00pm
5:30pm
6:00pm
6:30pm
7:00pm
7:30pm
8:00pm
8:30pm
9:00pm
9:30pm
10:00pm
10:30pm
11:00pm
11:30pm
12:00am

Plowed Roads At Nightfall

Hushed comes the dusk,
shadowed over snows,
over the good silos,
underneath the crows
that hope for mishap
and ceded bones.

The voiceless clouds
over windless plateaus,
over distant ice
static and cold,
over lifeless meadows
indifferent and frozen,

is this silence which echoes
as we drive towards the night.
It is tacit as rail fence
through acres divided.
It is boundaries in snow,
the ground fallow below
.

It's the dormant oak
on the mountain which glows
to silent siennas and lavender rose,
stunning the sky in Rococo
as the deaf air between us
sits monochrome.

44

Kiwanis Fair Closing

A carnival worker has slipped away
after engaging the gears of an empty ride.
He smokes in the forest away from his post.
He suddenly dies.
The carousel continues to spin
with no children, no sweet-hearts, nothing alive.
The calliope calls through the canopy,
steam pistons continue to drive:
fabric wrapped iron,
worn leather bridals,
grimaced faces in plaster of stallions
that spin and fall and rise
merrily in the night.

6:00am
6:30am
7:00am
7:30am
8:00am
8:30am
9:00am
9:30am
10:00am
10:30am
11:00am
11:30am
12:00pm
12:30pm
1:00pm
1:30pm
2:00pm
2:30pm
3:00pm
3:30pm
4:00pm
4:30pm
5:00pm
5:30pm
6:00pm
6:30pm
7:00pm
7:30pm
8:00pm
8:30pm
9:00pm
9:30pm
10:00pm
10:30pm
11:00pm
11:30pm
12:00am

6:00am
6:30am
7:00am
7:30am
8:00am
8:30am
9:00am
9:30am
10:00am
10:30am
11:00am
11:30am
12:00pm
12:30pm
1:00pm
1:30pm
2:00pm
2:30pm
3:00pm
3:30pm
4:00pm
4:30pm
5:00pm
5:30pm
6:00pm
6:30pm
7:00pm
7:30pm
8:00pm
8:30pm
9:00pm
9:30pm
10:00pm
10:30pm
11:00pm
11:30pm
12:00am

Holiday Concert

In the solemn stillness
of the grade school gym,
seraphic voices,
cherubic jazz hands,
blazers that hang low like cassocks,
sanctify us with innocence.
It is here that we worship
our last sacred thing;
these, our blessed offspring.

With phone lit faces beatified
by images of sons and daughters, we,
Attorney,
Sales Director,
Quant,
all of us who want for substance
in our mercenary days,
are addled sanctiloquents,
dazzled with awe, at what we have made.

The pretense of refined ennui,
the snark and civilized charm that flows
from pride we feel
in erudite lives,
is put to lie.
The passions towards our young on stage
are as primitive as shamans,
no matter how we try to hide.

So profane, the happy-houred father
seated at the end of the next row.
Still, he sits as if he sees a holy choir,
mouth pendent
searching for a word he does not know:
Ineffable? Sacral? Hallowed?
While I, back straight,
right thinking, fit, and secular,
gape ecstatic, like a Georgia snake handler.

Neverending Sunset
Munich To Newark With Jupiter

Clouds lavender for hours,
lie below but lie above
a purpled ocean tinted
by a sky where I am also
ten thousand meters high,
one thousand miles always east
from pallet-knifed horizons streaked
in stubborn orange changing
into passive blues from
dusk to dusk to dusk
to evening, only just one step
behind a prodigal sun,
below unlikely indigo
and pinned by Jove, which glows
so angry white, so sharp, above.

Thrum And Murmur

I can barely hear the tower bells
of the church up on the hill;
Congregational, two hundred years.

Only occasional in the night, I still complain
about the whistle of the diesel trains
sounding on the main commuter branch.

Airplane noise stays fairly distant,
but the inconsistent grumbles hinder,
any real indifference.

Persistent, but also random
is the whirr of wheels across macadam
in tandem with the endless purr of going somewhere else.

Phantoms wail through crevice with the wind,
and although I know it's just the wind,
the din beneath the quiet whisper,
whispers:
"might have been".

Distinguished

No upside to this growing old;
looking for silver linings
is like looking for gray pubic hairs
or at what's metastasized.

No upside
to constantly forgetting
what you felt you held so dear,
so soft;
a wedding day, grandchild's name,
a bucket list vacation gone away;
has all the money gone away?

How can you afford
to stay here at this quiet place
where all is tapioca beige
and everything
tastes like chicken?

That soothing hum?
The air conditioned sound
you'll hear the night you die.

There's too much time
too bad
you can't concentrate to read
or follow more than noises on the screens
that hover over every room.
Someone wants to see your stool.

6:00am
6:30am
7:00am
7:30am
8:00am
8:30am
9:00am
9:30am
10:00am
10:30am
11:00am
11:30am
12:00pm
12:30pm
1:00pm
1:30pm
2:00pm
2:30pm
3:00pm
3:30pm
4:00pm
4:30pm
5:00pm
5:30pm
6:00pm
6:30pm
7:00pm
7:30pm
8:00pm
8:30pm
9:00pm
9:30pm
10:00pm
10:30pm
11:00pm
11:30pm
12:00am

Tone Poem

The forest stands hard on suburban edge,
what light there is, is cloud reflected
from traffic lights at ghosted intersection,
closed up gas pumps, folded village.
I fancy this walk with the dog. Cold,
we each pretend we are alone.
He, hunting innocent, for innocent prey,
I with significant things to say
about guilt or transcendence or alienation,
or epiphanies of revelation—the dance
between moment and chaos
child and death, snowflake and frost.

The dog pees by a twig twisted hedge
in his own vain attempt to distinguish
one space from another.
I look at the darkness overhead.
What is the color of nighttime trees
as they forbid the nighttime sky...
the bark over stars and reluctant air...
the dark on dark, and black on bare...
the pigment between, barely implied?
Soft Denial, the name of the hues at midnight,
Tall-Shadow, the shade of the boughs which hide.
Yellow, the color of markings beside.

Tuesday Salut

So here's to all the fathers failed at
staying in their marriages,
inept but for the
reaching things,
and opening the mayonnaise.
We raise the glass from train-track flats,
darkened on a school-night with
flickered shadows, you-tube light, an iPhone,
and a fifth.

Pity Party

Exquisite the pity I plan for my part
: silent weeping in the dark.
Tallying slanders, summing betrayals,
egregious aggrievements
a list to enable,
ennoble,
ennui:
lamenting, regretting, conspicuous
me.